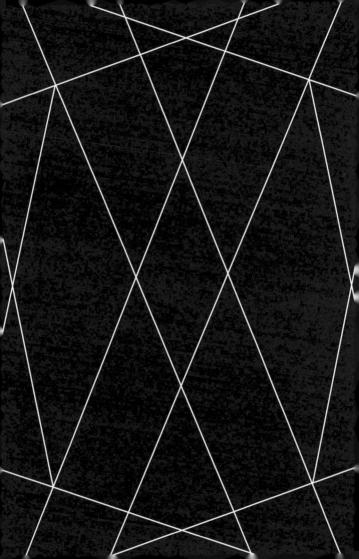

IT'S OK NOT TO BE OK

Good Advice and Kind Words for Positive Mental Well-Being

CLAIRE CHAMBERLAIN

IT'S OK NOT TO BE OK

An Hachette UK Company
www.hachette.co.uk

Vie Books, an imprint of Summersdale Publishers Ltd
Part of Octopus Publishing Group Limited
Carmelite House
50 Victoria Embankment
LONDON
EC4Y 0DZ
UK

www.summersdale.com

Printed and bound in China

ISBN: 978-1-78685-985-3

Substantial discounts on bulk quantities of Summersdale books are available to corporations, professional associations and other organizations. For details contact general enquiries: telephone: +44 (0) 1243 771107 or email: enquiries@summersdale.com.

Disclaimer
The author and the publisher cannot accept responsibility for any misuse or misunderstanding of any information contained herein, or any loss, damage or injury, be it health, financial or otherwise, suffered by any individual or group acting upon or relying on information contained herein. None of the views or suggestions in this book is intended to replace medical opinion from a doctor who is familiar with your particular circumstances. If you have concerns about your health, please seek professional advice.

INTRODUCTION

No one is happy all the time. In fact, it's perfectly normal to not feel OK sometimes. But whether you're just feeling a bit down, or you suspect it might be a more serious mental health problem, you should never feel like you have to go through a difficult period alone. As isolating as sadness, emptiness, anxiety or depression can feel, there are people who understand and care. This book is for anyone not feeling OK right now, for whatever reason. It's filled with practical tips and inspiring ideas to help you look after yourself when you're feeling low, as well as suggestions on where to find help if everything is getting too much, or you feel like you can no longer cope. I hope the following pages will help, and that they remind you that you are uniquely valuable – even when you might not feel like it.

NOT UNTIL WE ARE LOST DO WE BEGIN TO UNDERSTAND **OURSELVES**.

HENRY DAVID THOREAU

WHAT IS "OK", ANYWAY?

If you've ever been asked how you're feeling and have simply replied, "OK," without giving it much thought, you are certainly not alone. It's a reply that's uttered so frequently, it's almost become an expected response. But what if, underneath the surface, you really don't feel OK? And what's more, what if you don't feel it's OK to say you're not OK? Then take a deep breath and read on, because you are important... and so is your mental health.

THE MENTAL HEALTH SPECTRUM

Mental health is something everybody has. It exists on a spectrum and, as with your physical health, it needs to be nurtured if it's to be kept in good condition. Sometimes, however, you can do as much nurturing as you like, but you might still experience mental health difficulties. This can happen for a variety of reasons, from a sudden life event, to a hormonal imbalance, to an underlying mental health condition.

Experiencing a mental health problem can feel lonely, and you might think no one else has ever felt the way you do. But however isolated you might feel, it's important to recognize that these feelings affect most people at some point in their lives – the World Health Organization (WHO) states that one in four people will experience mental health difficulties at some stage. It's also perfectly normal to feel low or flat sometimes. But if your poor mental health is stopping you from living your life as you would wish – for example, if you're struggling to get out of bed in the morning, or you're experiencing chronic anxiety – it's important to address the issue, to help ease your distress and stop it from escalating.

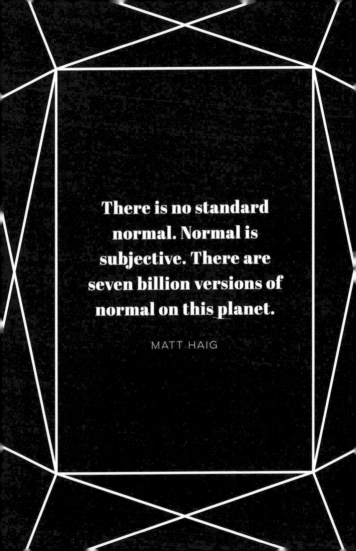

There is no standard normal. Normal is subjective. There are seven billion versions of normal on this planet.

MATT HAIG

YOU ARE
NOT ON
YOUR OWN.

Accept that you are perfectly imperfect

When you're struggling with your mental health, it can feel like an exhausting battle as you try to fight demons and wrestle negative emotions. So, if life is feeling hard, it's time to take some gentle, positive action. The first step (which can be the hardest) is to accept yourself, in this moment, exactly as you are. You might feel low; you might be suffering with anxiety; you might be living with depression, or struggling with an addiction. But right now you are still a whole and necessary human being… "imperfections" and all.

EMBRACE THE GLORIOUS MESS THAT YOU ARE.

ELIZABETH GILBERT

You deserve better

Freeing yourself from states of depression, stress, anxiety, sadness, poor mood or low self-worth is hard. Living with any of the above (or any other mental health condition) can make you feel helpless, and the longer it goes on, the less you might feel that you deserve happiness, contentment or love. However, feeling undeserving can create unconscious resistance to growth and positive change. This means that, no matter how much you want things to change, you might get stuck in a cycle of self-sabotage. It may seem tough, but in order to move forwards and create a more positive, nurturing mindset, you need to forgive yourself. Yes, there may be pain in your past – be it loss, trauma, shame, regret or anger – but in order to allow yourself to move on, you now need to be gentle with yourself. View yourself through a more compassionate lens: you are human, and humans experience pain and make mistakes. By forgiving yourself for past actions, thoughts and emotions you make room for empowering and positive change.

You are
enough.
Always.

UNDERSTANDING MENTAL HEALTH ISSUES

Mental health problems affect one in four adults at some point in their lives, so rest assured that if you're struggling right now, you are not alone, even if that is how you feel. It's a sad fact that many people suffer in silence, because of the perceived stigma surrounding mental health issues. But whatever thoughts, feelings, emotions or behaviours you are experiencing, trust in the fact that you are not "weird" or "different". You are a normal person coping with a challenging condition... and you are stronger than you know.

What causes mental health problems?

Poor mental health can have a wide range of causes; for many people, there is often more than one trigger. Mental health problems may be related to any number of factors, including childhood trauma, loss or bereavement, redundancy or unemployment, financial worries, loneliness or social isolation, living with a chronic physical illness, experiencing trauma as an adult, being a carer for a loved one, or physical or genetic causes. Whatever the reason, there is no shame in your suffering, nor should you blame yourself for it – and there are lots of ways to improve your mental well-being.

NEVER GIVE UP ON YOURSELF.

How are mental health problems diagnosed?

It might feel difficult or uncomfortable, but if you are experiencing poor mental health, it's really important to speak to someone. In the first instance, this might be a loved one or someone you trust. But you might then need to speak to a trained counsellor or a doctor. A doctor will ask you a range of questions relating to your mood, emotions and behaviours. If your symptoms relate to a common condition, such as anxiety, they will be able to diagnose you. If, however, your symptoms relate to a more complex problem, you might be referred to a specialist. Again, this is nothing to feel scared about, and will simply mean you will get the best professional help available.

**Don't allow your
wounds to transform
you into a person
you are not.**

PAULO COELHO

STRESS

While it's not an illness in itself, stress can feel
uncomfortable and even debilitating, and it's
often a precursor to more severe mental health
difficulties. Stress is the feeling of being unable
to cope in the face of mental or emotional
pressure. This pressure can come from work,
financial or relationship concerns, or any
number of other life demands, and when you
begin to feel like you can't cope, this sense
of helplessness can actually get in the way of
dealing with these pressures. Stress can cause
mental anguish, such as worry and anxiety,
but because stress releases hormones in the

body that trigger the "fight, flight or freeze" response, there will also be a physical reaction to the stress. This often manifests as raised blood pressure and shallow breathing, and can result in headaches, pain or muscle tension. You may also find your behaviour changes – for example, you might lose your temper more easily or resort to alcohol to try to dull sensations. When the cause of your stress passes, the symptoms will ease, but if you feel constantly unable to cope with the pressures you are under, this can lead to chronic stress, for which you should seek professional help.

PEACE CAN
BECOME A LENS
THROUGH WHICH
YOU SEE THE
WORLD. BE IT.
LIVE IT.

WAYNE DYER

Anger

Everyone feels angry sometimes. In fact, anger is a perfectly normal, healthy emotion that we experience in the face of frustration, deceit, or inequality. But if anger becomes uncontrollable, harming both you and those around you, it's a problem. If you regularly experience aggressive outbursts (either verbal or physical), if you feel your anger is blocking out other emotions, or if you turn your anger on yourself, leading to self-hatred, this may need to be addressed, with self-help techniques or professional guidance.

Anxiety

Anxiety is often characterized by a feeling of worry, dread or impending doom, usually in relation to a future event (or something you think might happen). Most people experience some level of anxiety at times – perhaps before a big work presentation, or during a period of change. Anxiety becomes a mental health condition when it starts to affect the way you live your life. For example, if your anxiety is fairly constant, or your fears are out of proportion to the situation, or you start avoiding certain situations because of your anxiety, it could well be a problem. Symptoms are often both mental and physical, and include feeling tense and unable to relax, thinking that bad things will happen, feelings of dissociation (e.g. feeling disconnected from your body), needing constant reassurance, "butterflies" in your stomach, feeling nauseous, headaches, dizziness and shallow breathing.

Sometimes, the physical effects are so severe that you may worry you have an undiagnosed illness. If you recognize any of these symptoms, it's best to visit your doctor. Depending on the type of symptoms you are experiencing, you might be diagnosed with an anxiety disorder, such as generalized anxiety disorder (uncontrollable worry relating to many aspects of everyday life) or social anxiety disorder (fear triggered by social settings).

WORRY PRETENDS TO
BE NECESSARY BUT
SERVES NO USEFUL
PURPOSE.

ECKHART TOLLE

You're not the only one going through this.

DEPRESSION

Depression is characterized by a low mood that you just can't shift. It exists on a spectrum. Mild depression might see you feeling sad or low and, while life may feel less worthwhile or more difficult, you can still go about your day-to-day activities. Severe depression, however, is extremely serious, leading to suicidal thoughts and a sense that life just isn't worth living any more. Those who are able to talk about their depression often describe feeling empty or numb – of having no energy and experiencing no real emotion, either positive or negative. You might feel tired all the time, struggle to think with clarity, struggle to make contact with friends or loved ones, drink or smoke more than usual, or experience feelings of hopelessness or worthlessness. The symptoms of depression can make it hard to tell someone what's going on, but if you can communicate how you're feeling to a loved one, it can help. It's also important to care for yourself during times when you are feeling low or depressed.

HOPE SHINES
BRIGHTEST IN
THE DARKEST
OF MOMENTS.

Panic attacks

A panic attack can feel terrifying. It is an abrupt onset of intense fear and can last for anywhere between 5 and 20 minutes – sometimes even longer. During a panic attack, symptoms often build up very quickly and can include a racing heart, shallow breath, trembling, sweating, chest pain and a fear that you are going to collapse. A panic attack is not physically dangerous in itself, but if you are in the middle of one, it can be very real and frightening. If you find yourself experiencing a panic attack, it may help to focus on breathing as slowly and deeply as you can.

HANG IN THERE — YOU WILL BE FINE.

Alcohol or drug abuse

All drugs, whether legal (such as alcohol) or otherwise, have the potential to affect your mental health. If you become dependent on alcohol or drugs, you are likely to experience other negative consequences, including physical and social problems. You might turn to alcohol or drugs in an attempt to mask underlying issues. Whatever the reason, if you're concerned about the amount you are drinking, it's important to get support, whether that's first telling someone close to you or seeking professional medical advice.

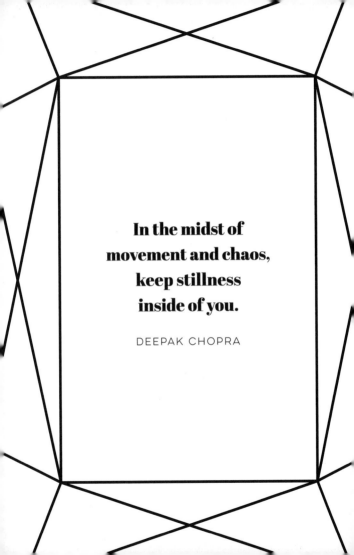

**In the midst of
movement and chaos,
keep stillness
inside of you.**

DEEPAK CHOPRA

DO ONE
SMALL THING
TODAY THAT
MAKES YOU
HAPPY.

FEELING LOW

Generally feeling sad, down or a bit low is very common. You might know the cause of your low mood – perhaps you're experiencing a tough time at work, going through a relationship break-up, struggling to sleep at night or dealing with a chronic illness. Sometimes, though, you might feel down but not really know the cause. It's important to be kind to yourself during times of low mood: eat well, drink lots of water, rest, get some fresh air and remember to treat yourself. If your low mood continues for more than a couple of weeks, or gets worse, you may be experiencing signs of depression. Keep being as kind to yourself as possible, and try to open up to someone close to you. It's also a good idea to make an appointment with your doctor, who will be able to listen to what you've been going through and offer impartial advice on how best to move forward.

Disordered eating and eating disorders

Many people believe that eating disorders stem from a desire to be slim, but often this is not the case. Eating disorders are complex mental illnesses. There's no single cause, but they can often stem from feelings of low self-esteem, control issues, anxiety, depression, perfectionism, high-pressure environments (often the pressure is self-inflicted) or bullying. Those on the autistic spectrum may also be susceptible. The term "eating disorders" refers to illnesses that can be diagnosed with a specific set of criteria, such as anorexia nervosa, bulimia nervosa or binge-eating disorder. "Disordered eating", on the other hand, is a descriptive term that refers to problems with food that fall outside these criteria. It's still serious, and may include symptoms such as chronic weight fluctuations, rigid rules about food, meal skipping and feelings of shame associated with eating.

Both eating disorders and disordered eating have serious mental and physical consequences, which can be life-threatening. If you suspect you have a problem with eating, it's important to open up to someone, even though this can feel very scary. Eating disorders tend to go hand in hand with secrecy – many keep the problem to themselves for fear that their symptoms are not severe enough to warrant attention. But all sufferers are worthy of support and it's vital to get professional guidance.

YOU CAN DO ANYTHING, BUT NOT EVERYTHING.

DAVID ALLEN

You
are
good
enough.

Self-injury

Self-injury (such as cutting, bruising or burning yourself) is often thought of by others as suicidal behaviour, but in reality this is normally not the case. It's generally used as a coping mechanism – a way of relieving the tension, pressure and emotional pain which might otherwise escalate. Those who hurt themselves usually have a strong desire to live. However, self-harm can be upsetting, for both the sufferer and loved ones who are aware of the behaviour, and it does not address the underlying emotional issues that are causing the internal distress. Professional guidance can help you deal with these issues and learn how to cope without hurting yourself.

It's never
overreacting
to ask for what you
want and need.

AMY POEHLER

SUICIDAL FEELINGS

If you are feeling suicidal, please seek help immediately. Call a friend or loved one, or go to see them if they are nearby. If you are alone or wish to remain anonymous, there are 24-hour services you can call for support, including The Samaritans (turn to the Resources section of this book for details). Suicidal feelings are normally the result of many months of feeling helpless and despairing. They can range from thoughts about how you might end your life, to feeling like you can no longer go on leading the life you are living, to thinking that other people might be better off without you. You may feel like you will never be happy again. But it's important to remember that, however all-consuming and overwhelming they can feel, suicidal thoughts do not last forever. You can move past them and go on to lead a happy and fulfilling life. Always remember that you are not alone. You are loved, and you are worthy of guidance and support.

A note on social media

For many people, social media has become a normal part of everyday life. Logging on to an Instagram or Facebook account, for example, is viewed as a good way to "interact" with others. However, numerous studies have found that high social media use can result in poor mental health, and the more time users spend on social media, the more likely they are to experience symptoms of depression, anxiety, "fear of missing out" (FOMO) or lower self-esteem.

When viewed with a relaxed mindset, for a short amount of time each day, social media can be an effective way to connect with like-minded people. Unfortunately, though, it's easy to begin checking social media obsessively, getting sucked into a cycle of social comparison. It's important to remember that social media is not real life: it's a highly edited (and often filtered) snapshot of the moments people want you to see.

If social media is starting to make you feel unhappy, consider whether it might be better to curb your time on it. Try limiting yourself to half an hour a day for a few weeks, or have a couple of social-media-free days each week, and see if you feel differently afterwards.

VERY LITTLE IS
NEEDED TO MAKE
A HAPPY LIFE;
IT IS ALL WITHIN
YOURSELF, IN
YOUR WAY OF
THINKING.

MARCUS AURELIUS

BE KIND TO YOUR BODY

Your mental and physical well-being are intrinsically linked. Exercising and eating a healthy, balanced diet are things we often associate only with physical health, but they are also vital for your mental health. And it's not just your fitness and diet that have an impact. Other aspects of your lifestyle, including the amount of alcohol you drink and how much sleep you get, also play an important part in staying both physically and mentally healthy. Over the following pages, we will look at some gentle, holistic ways you can ensure your day-to-day living is supporting your goal of improved mental wellness.

A note on healthy, balanced eating

It's a fairly common misconception that healthy eating involves some form of deprivation: that you'll miss out on foods you love, or won't be able to indulge every so often. On the contrary, eating a healthy, balanced diet is not actually a "diet" at all – it's simply a way of eating that helps to support your overall health. "Healthy" just means providing your body with the nutrients it needs to maintain your energy, immunity and optimum brain function, while "balanced" means eating a broad range of foods – including the odd treat when you fancy!

When eating for good health, it's a great idea to include a wide variety of fruit and vegetables (aim for five portions a day); carbohydrates, such as wholegrain bread; healthy fats, like salmon or avocado; and protein, such as lean meat, fish, seafood, eggs, beans or tofu. And of course, in any balanced diet it's fine to have a treat, so enjoy that slice of cake or savour a few squares of chocolate. The key with treats is to eat them more mindfully, by relishing every mouthful, so you truly appreciate them and don't need to overindulge. Enjoy!

You
can
start
right
now.

Eat more good fats

Your brain needs a regular supply of essential fatty acids (EFAs) to help maintain its health and keep it functioning well. These types of fats are called "essential" because your body can't make them, so you have to include them in your diet. These "good" fats, such as omega-3, can be found in a whole host of foods, including oily fish (such as salmon and mackerel), avocados, nuts (especially walnuts and almonds), olives and olive oil, chia seeds and flaxseeds. Try to avoid artificially made trans fats, which are found in many processed foods, as these are damaging for your health.

LET FOOD BE THY MEDICINE AND MEDICINE BE THY FOOD.

HIPPOCRATES

Boost your vitamin B intake

B vitamins are especially important in helping to regulate your mood. If you're feeling low, try boosting your intake of these vital vitamins, which play a key role in the production of serotonin – the neurotransmitter thought to contribute to feelings of well-being and happiness.

B vitamins can be found in wholegrains, dark green leafy vegetables, beans, peanuts, eggs, avocados, yeast extract, poultry, liver, dairy products and fortified cereals.

SMALL STEPS ALL ADD UP.

**Take care
of your body.
It's the only place
you have to live.**

JIM ROHN

Opt for wholesome comfort foods

Instead of opting for unhealthy, processed and shop-bought comfort foods, high in trans fats and low in goodness, spend a little time preparing your own hearty, nourishing and soul-warming options. Think bowls of colourful spicy curries, warming soups, filling stews from your childhood, fresh and fragrant rainbow salads and zingy, fruit-packed smoothies. Homemade food is definitely good for the body… and mind.

IT MIGHT
NOT BE
EASY, BUT
IT WILL BE
WORTH IT.

TRY TO AVOID ALCOHOL

If you find yourself turning to alcohol to help you unwind, you're certainly not alone. While alcohol can initially induce relaxation, this is short-lived and more often than not outweighed by the negative consequences, which can include disturbed sleep, anxiety, depression, fatigue and feeling less able to cope with everyday life.

Perhaps you feel that you may have a problem with alcohol? Realizing this can be scary, but it's an important first step. If you are concerned you may be depending on alcohol too often, or if a relative or friend has raised the issue of your drinking habits with you, it may be a good idea to address this. Spend a little time considering the ways in which alcohol is influencing your day-to-day life. If you notice it's having an impact on your work or social life, or if it's affecting your relationships, you could create an action plan. Do you want to stop drinking on certain days of the week, or quit altogether? When are you going to start? Be specific. Let others know your goal – this will make you accountable, and will also provide a ready-made support system, should you need it.

I am strong, capable and confident.

IT'S NOT SELFISH
TO LOVE YOURSELF,
TAKE CARE OF
YOURSELF, AND TO
MAKE YOUR HAPPINESS
A PRIORITY. IT'S
NECESSARY.

MANDY HALE

Get out in the fresh air

Spending time in the natural world has been shown to provide a host of mental health benefits, including helping to reduce feelings of anxiety and stress, and even alleviating mild to moderate depression. In fact, it's so beneficial that in recent years, ecotherapy (also known as green therapy) has become a recognized therapeutic treatment. Spending time in the great outdoors can boost your sense of well-being, positivity and resilience, and the peaceful setting can lead to feelings of gratitude, acceptance and mindfulness, all of which can result in a calmer, more positive outlook.

Being outdoors is also a wonderful opportunity to feel the sun on your skin – important for the production of vitamin D and mood-boosting serotonin. If you're feeling low, the thought of heading out and about can feel overwhelming or exhausting, but if you're not up to a long walk, even sitting in a sunny spot in a garden or park for 5 minutes, with a cup of tea and a book, can bring some big wellness benefits. See if you can immerse yourself in the joys of the outside world in some small way every day.

Drink a glass of water

Drinking enough water is vital to help you stay mentally focused, boost your concentration levels and mood, and even help stave off anxiety and fatigue. So if you're feeling low, off or irritable, something as simple as drinking a glass of water could help you feel a bit better. It's recommended that you drink between six and eight glasses a day. Try adding mint leaves, lemon wedges or cucumber slices for flavour – and remember, juices, herbal teas, and even black tea and coffee all count, too.

I'VE
GOT THIS.

Try forest bathing

Shinrin-yoku, which translates as "forest bathing", is a practice that was developed in Japan in the 1980s, and which has now been embraced by Japanese healthcare. It involves simply spending time sitting in (or walking slowly through) a woodland or forest, to allow your mind and body to be both immersed in, and to reconnect with, the natural world. The practice is beginning to be introduced into Western cultures, and the list of benefits is extensive: *shinrin-yoku* is a wonderful way to reduce stress, lower blood pressure, improve energy levels, boost your mood, and promote a deep sense of contentment.

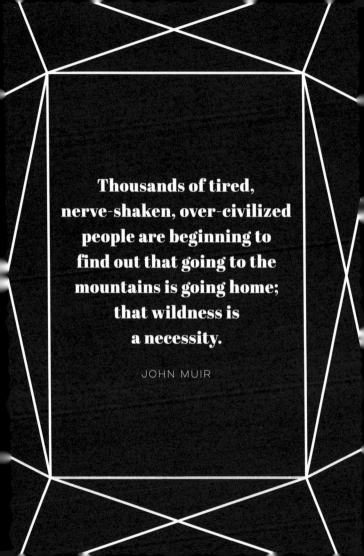

Thousands of tired, nerve-shaken, over-civilized people are beginning to find out that going to the mountains is going home; that wildness is a necessity.

JOHN MUIR

Get your heart racing

It's well documented that exercise is a wonderful way to promote both good physical and mental health, with some doctors now prescribing physical activity to help alleviate symptoms of mild to moderate depression. Exercise is also proven to help reduce stress and anxiety, and to boost feelings of confidence, resilience, self-esteem and happiness. How? As well as flooding your body with endorphins (the happy hormone), exercising is a fantastic way of discovering just how much your body is capable of (often it's a lot more than you realize). And the fitter and stronger you become, the more capable and empowered you start to feel.

When you first begin to exercise, it's important to start small: perhaps head out for a 15-minute walk each day, then slowly build up, or follow a beginner's jogging plan. Set yourself small, achievable goals, and truly appreciate each achievement as you reach it. It's important to get your heart racing when you exercise, so whatever you do – be it brisk walking, jogging, cycling or swimming – include regular intervals where you move at a faster pace, to really reap the full benefits.

Choose exercise you enjoy

When aiming to increase your activity levels, it's important to pick a fitness pursuit that makes you happy. Choose something you love, and you'll be more likely to stick with it. If you're nervous about exercising with others, perhaps brisk walking or jogging on your own might be a good start. If you'd love to join a gym but don't know how the machines work, why not book some sessions with a personal trainer, who will be able to guide you? And think outside the box! Have you considered boxing, cycling, climbing, horse riding, yoga or paddle boarding? There really is something for everyone.

WORK OUT
BECAUSE
YOU LOVE
YOUR BODY,
NOT BECAUSE
YOU HATE IT.

MOVE
A LITTLE
MORE

Improving your physical fitness is not simply about set sessions of structured exercise. All the daily movement you do counts. While it can feel hard to exercise when you're in a dark place mentally, getting up, out and about will go a long way towards boosting your mental health. Make it your aim to move a little more throughout each and every day, by making small changes to your daily routine that will have a big impact on your physical health and mood. For example, walk short distances instead of driving, take the stairs at work, get off the train or bus a stop early and walk the rest of your journey, head for a lunchtime stroll instead of sitting at your desk or on the sofa, and get up regularly to stretch and move around if your day is mostly sedentary. Your body and mind will thank you for it.

Stretch yourself

Giving yourself a physical and mental boost might be as simple as spending a few minutes gently stretching your body. As well as increasing blood flow to your muscles, a good stretch also releases endorphins into your bloodstream. And to top it off, gentle, static stretches (stretches that you hold for several minutes or more) activate your parasympathetic nervous system, which helps to invoke a sense of deep relaxation.

EVERY DAY BRINGS
A CHANCE FOR
YOU TO DRAW IN
A BREATH, KICK
OFF YOUR SHOES,
AND **DANCE.**

OPRAH WINFREY

Treat yourself to a massage

A massage is a wonderful way to care for yourself and, as well as offering numerous physical benefits, including improved circulation, there are also a host of mental benefits, too. Regular massage has been shown to ease stress and even alleviate mild to moderate depression, so it's the perfect all-rounder to help promote relaxation. Booking a session with a professional massage therapist is a fabulous gift for yourself, but a massage from a partner can also be a good method of stress relief. Alternatively, try some self-massage: rolling the soles of your feet over a tennis ball is an easy way to ease tension.

My body is amazing.

Try a few yoga poses

There are many proven benefits of a regular yoga practice, including improved strength, flexibility and posture, reduced stress, increased energy, greater happiness and improved concentration. Essentially a spiritual practice, yoga blends a series of postures (asanas) with breathing (pranayama) and meditation, helping to evoke a sense of calm, peace and stillness within. While you have the option of practising yoga in the comfort of your own home, it's a good idea to seek professional guidance from a fully qualified instructor when you're first starting out, as they will be able to lead you through the poses safely. Contrary to many myths, yoga is not simply for the super-flexible, and you will find a whole array of abilities and body shapes at yoga classes, so don't be nervous – yoga really is for everyone.

Yoga teaches us to cure what need not be endured and endure what cannot be cured.

B. K. S. IYENGAR

I AM
BRAVE.

Enjoy a better night's sleep

Sleep is a vital physiological process that restores both your mind and body. Lack of sleep can increase feelings of stress and anxiety, as well as impairing your concentration and judgement, so making sure you get enough is crucial for your overall well-being. Experts are in agreement that 8 hours of shut-eye is about the right amount for most adults – although you will likely need to be in bed for a little longer to ensure you achieve that amount. If you struggle to drift off to sleep, try implementing a relaxing and nurturing bedtime routine each evening. Aim to avoid using electronic devices in the hour before bed, as the blue light they emit alters your levels of sleep-inducing melatonin. Instead, try taking a warm bath, using a lavender-scented moisturizer, popping on some cosy pyjamas, reading a book or trying 10 minutes of meditation.

SLEEP IS
THE GOLDEN
CHAIN THAT TIES
HEALTH AND OUR
BODIES TOGETHER.

THOMAS DEKKER

I DESERVE
CARE AND
LOVE.

Soak in the bath

A relaxing soak in a warm bath is a wonderful way to switch off, unwind and relieve any stress or physical tension you may be feeling in your body. It's also good for your mind and soul. Light some candles to set a soothing, restorative mood, and add your favourite bath oil for a touch of luxury. If your muscles feel particularly tense, swap the bath oil for a scoop of Epsom salts to ease away aches and pains. Don't have much time? A hot shower can work wonders, too.

BE KIND TO
YOUR MIND

Taking a little time out of each and every day to check in with your mind is an important step to help protect and preserve your mental health. Some days it might simply be a few moments to connect with the silence behind your thoughts; other times you might have longer to dedicate to your mental well-being. The following pages offer numerous ways you can be kind to your mind, whether you have a few seconds or a whole day.

Understanding automatic thinking

The average person has anything up to 70,000 thoughts each day. That's a lot of internal chatter to contend with. It's no wonder so many of us find the concept of inner peace somewhat elusive. The majority of these thoughts are automatic, which means we're not even fully conscious of them. They simply buzz around our heads creating noise – narrating, interpreting, judging. The thoughts are created by your brain to help you make sense of the world around you, but some of them can become intrusive, especially if you are prone to negative thinking. It may sound strange, but you don't have to believe everything you think. Realizing this can be a weight off your mind.

CHANGE YOUR THOUGHTS AND YOU CHANGE YOUR **WORLD.**

NORMAN VINCENT PEALE

YOU ARE NOT YOUR THOUGHTS

Becoming aware of the fact that you are not your thoughts is a powerful and very freeing realization. All that internal noise and chatter, the constant narrating, judging and accusing… it is not you. To fully understand this, find a time when you can be alone for 10 minutes or so, and sit quietly. Take a few deep breaths and then begin to draw your attention to your thoughts. Really listen to that voice inside your head. What is it saying? Often it will simply be narrating what is going on around you, but it may also be voicing your worries and anxieties, or replaying scenes from the past, or possible future scenarios that have not yet happened. Notice and observe these, without judging them or trying to change them. This will make it easier to accept the following: if you can notice your thoughts as an observer, then you are not your thoughts. And noticing them allows you to also appreciate the deep calm and silence behind your thoughts. Whenever your inner voice gets too loud, simply stop and notice the thoughts *as thoughts*.

Stop the cycle

If you're struggling to escape a cycle of
negative or anxious thoughts, sometimes
simply noticing them may not be enough to
break their hold over you. In these instances,
you might need to physically do something
to distract yourself away from them. Saying
"Stop it!" out loud can sometimes help, but
find something that works for you: jog on
the spot for 30 seconds, do 20 star jumps,
blast the radio and dance for a few minutes –
anything that distracts you from the negative
thought pattern.

THIS TOO WILL PASS.

Forgive yourself – and others

Holding on to resentment is a surefire way to experience mental unrest. Constantly berating yourself for past mistakes, or holding a grudge against someone else, is neither helpful nor constructive. In fact, it is actually damaging and draining. You are human, and humans make mistakes. Gently accept your humanness, and the humanness of those around you, by forgiving past behaviours and moving on. Learn from the past, but don't hold onto it. This moment, right now, is a fresh start.

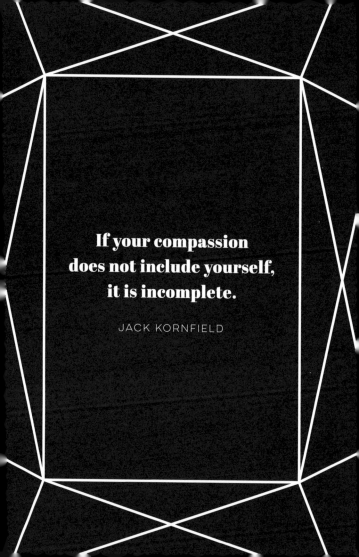

**If your compassion
does not include yourself,
it is incomplete.**

JACK KORNFIELD

FACE
YOUR
FEARS

Pushing any fears or worries you may have to the back of your mind will most likely lead to a feeling of free-floating anxiety and a nagging sense that something is bothering you. You may also find the worries play out in your subconscious, either through recurring dreams at night, or through certain behaviours. You might, for example, find yourself snapping at friends or family for no fault of their own, because you're too scared to face up to the worries or emotions inside you. Confronting your fears can seem scary or even mentally painful, but you are likely to find that bringing them into your conscious mind and taking the necessary steps to deal with them will remove their power. What are the real issues that are concerning you? Write them down and then consider some actions you could take to overcome them. Is something from your past stopping you from moving on with your life? Is it something you can deal with alone? Would it help to open up to a friend? Might it be a good idea to seek professional advice? By actively working towards overcoming your fears, their significance will diminish.

Accept the uncertainty of life

Uncertainty can often make us feel uneasy: not knowing what is just around the corner can lead to a sense of vulnerability. However, much of our lives truly is uncertain – none of us really knows what is in store, and no matter how much planning you do, life will often throw you a curveball when you least expect it. Accepting and embracing this truth can be a liberating feeling. Shifting your mindset is helpful: try viewing uncertainty as exciting, rather than worrying. And instead of attempting to control every situation, accept that often it's OK to not know exactly what lies ahead.

Trust in this new beginning.

Cease judgement

Judging yourself negatively by criticizing your own actions, thoughts or appearance, or by constantly comparing yourself to others, is a highly self-destructive habit that only serves to undermine your confidence and sense of self-worth. While it's true that some forms of judgement are necessary (logical judgements can help keep you safe or achieve a goal, for example), it's important that these judgements come from a place of self-love rather than self-loathing. If you regularly find yourself berating yourself, telling yourself you "should" be better, happier or more accomplished, it will only lead to more misery.

To help stop self-judging, first notice when it happens. As soon as a judgemental thought arises, ask yourself the following questions: is it helpful or serving a purpose? Would I say this to a friend or loved one? If the answer is no, acknowledge the judgement but don't engage with it – simply let it go. By acknowledging your negative judgements but then moving on, rather than getting caught up in them, you will gradually start to become kinder to yourself.

It's not selfish to do what's best for you.

IF YOU DON'T
LIKE SOMETHING,
CHANGE IT.
IF YOU CAN'T
CHANGE IT,
CHANGE YOUR
ATTITUDE.

MAYA ANGELOU

Stop battling what "is"

Accepting life exactly as it is, rather than wishing circumstances were different, is an important step. One thing you can almost never control is the external events that happen to you. But you can always control your behaviour in relation to these events. If you constantly blame your mood on circumstances beyond your control, you'll feel powerless. Conversely, starting to take responsibility for the way you respond to these circumstances by acting more positively, even in the face of big challenges, can be hugely empowering.

I WILL STEP
INTO EACH DAY
WITH COURAGE
AND POSITIVITY.

WHAT MATTERS
MOST IS HOW WELL
YOU WALK THROUGH
THE **FIRE.**

CHARLES BUKOWSKI

"Behave" yourself happy

Research has found that even a forced, fake smile decreases stress levels and makes you feel brighter. So why not try "acting" happy? Think about how you usually behave when you're contented, such as cooking yourself a nutritious and delicious meal, getting outside for a walk, treating yourself to a small gift and smiling more. Start doing these things even when you're feeling low – they are all small gestures, but they will make a big difference.

FIND A HAPPY PLACE

If you struggle with poor mental health and find it difficult to switch off worries or negative thoughts, visualization could help you through tough moments. Utilizing mental imagery in this way has been shown to calm the mind, help regulate breathing, and reduce feelings of stress and anxiety. One of the easiest visualization techniques is to think of a place that makes you feel calm and relaxed, and imagine you are there. It could be a warm tropical beach, an alpine meadow, a mountaintop with an epic view, or the sunny terrace of a

Mediterranean villa – whatever appeals to you most.

To begin, gently close your eyes and take a few deep breaths, then mentally immerse yourself in your chosen surroundings. What can you see, hear and smell? Can you feel the warmth of the sun on your skin, or a gentle breeze? Imagine any tension dropping away from your body. When you are ready, gently open your eyes and bring yourself back to the present moment, retaining the sense of peace. This relaxing haven is available to you in your mind whenever you need to go there.

Identify your triggers

Start paying attention to episodes of anxiety, sadness and stress. Is there a pattern playing out for you? Some might be obvious – for example, being in large crowds or public speaking – but others are perhaps less so. By spending a little time identifying the situations and events that trigger you, you may be able to start managing and addressing them more effectively.

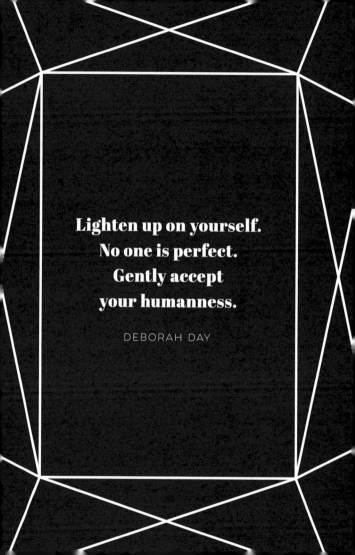

Lighten up on yourself.
No one is perfect.
Gently accept
your humanness.

DEBORAH DAY

I WILL BE KIND TO MYSELF TODAY.

Cultivate positivity

People with an optimistic outlook tend to cultivate positivity within their lives each and every day, until looking on the bright side has become a habit. To start doing the same, look for positives in ordinary daily activities. Notice the way the sun shines through the clouds as you walk to the shops, or the feel of the hot water on your skin in your morning shower. Spending time with positive people is also a good way to boost positivity, so if you're up to it, call one of your most optimistic friends for a chat or arrange to meet them.

Write it down

Keeping a journal can be incredibly cathartic – the process of putting thoughts onto paper helps to calm your mind, and it may even clarify feelings and emotions that you have found difficult to express, or even name. There are many different writing options that may help – journaling your thoughts, feelings and behaviours in a diary is one method – and this can help you notice patterns or triggers. Or try writing down the things that have been bothering or upsetting you, screwing them up and throwing them away – a physical representation of letting go of negativity.

I am calm, peaceful and relaxed.

ALMOST
EVERYTHING
WILL WORK
AGAIN IF YOU
UNPLUG IT FOR
A FEW MINUTES,
INCLUDING YOU.

ANNE LAMOTT

Press pause

If life is getting on top of you, pause…
literally. Interrupt your thoughts by taking
a deep breath and counting slowly to ten.
It might only be a brief respite, but in that
short moment you will give yourself a little
space and time to calm your mind and
counteract the overwhelming sensations
you have been experiencing.

Become more mindful

Mindfulness is the act of becoming consciously aware of the present moment exactly as it is – of your body, thoughts, feelings and the world around you – without judgement. It's a way of reconnecting with the "now" without worries or anxieties crowding your mind – all of which stop you experiencing the present fully and consciously. Drawing your attention to the present moment is as simple as it sounds but it can take practice, so don't be hard on yourself if you struggle at first.

When starting out, it might be easier to pick a time when you feel calm and alert – observe your surroundings, your bodily sensations and any feelings you may be experiencing. If you notice a thought arise that takes your mind away from the present moment, acknowledge it without judgement, then draw your attention back to "now". In time, mindfulness can help you become comfortable with difficult situations. Also, by helping to draw you out of your mind and back to your physical body and the world you inhabit, it can greatly improve your well-being in times of mental distress.

Try meditating

Studies have shown that meditation can have powerful positive effects on both your mind and body, reducing stress, lowering heart rate and blood pressure, improving circulation and boosting overall well-being. Essentially, meditation is simply focused attention without judgement – for example, attention on the breath, on the body or on an external object, such as a candle flame. When you first start, it may feel awkward and mentally uncomfortable, but as with anything, the more you practise, the more natural it will become. There are many guided meditations online to help you.

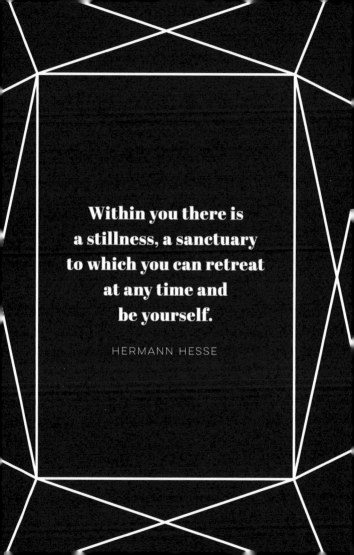

**Within you there is
a stillness, a sanctuary
to which you can retreat
at any time and
be yourself.**

HERMANN HESSE

INHALE FULLY, EXHALE SLOWLY.

Breathe more deeply

Taking long, slow, deep breaths is a centuries-old technique used to help counteract feelings of stress and anxiety. It works by interrupting the sympathetic nervous system (which produces the body's "fight, flight or freeze" response), instead triggering the parasympathetic nervous system, which invokes a sense of relaxation and calm. It's so simple and effective that you can do it anywhere: every time you start to feel overwhelmed, anxious, nervous, tense or stressed, start inhaling deeply, from the pit of your stomach up to the top of your lungs, then exhale slowly, relaxing your shoulders as you do so.

Perform a body scan

Often we get so caught up in our minds that we end up with a feeling of free-floating anxiety. This short meditation can help you feel more grounded, by drawing your attention back to your physical body. To start, find a quiet place and sit or lie comfortably. Then draw your attention to your feet. How do they feel? Hot or cold? Relaxed or tense? Notice any sensations, without judgement. Slowly draw your attention up through all areas of the body, noticing, but without trying to change anything. The result is frequently a feeling of calm.

I AM
WORTHY OF
AFFECTION AND
UNDERSTANDING.

If you want to conquer the anxiety of life, live in the moment, live in the breath.

AMIT RAY

Try reflexology

Reflexology is based on the premise that there are reflexes in your feet (and also your hands and ears) that correspond to every part of the body. A reflexologist will use pressure-point massage to stimulate these reflexes, which is said to improve nerve function and blood flow. Studies have also shown that the relaxing practice of reflexology can help to alleviate stress, anxiety and even depression.

USE ESSENTIAL OILS

Aromatherapy has a long tradition as a powerful alternative therapy, and is used to help with a wide range of mental, emotional and physical health issues. Studies have shown that the use of certain essential oils can help to alleviate anxiety, ease mild depression, lower stress levels, aid a more restful night's sleep and promote feelings of joy. Some of the best-known oils to aid good mental health include bergamot, lavender, ylang-ylang, rose and chamomile.

There are a variety of ways to use essential oils, so choose whichever option feels most comfortable for you. You can try inhalation, by applying a few drops to a tissue or pillow at night and gently breathing in the aroma. They can also be applied directly to the skin, mixing them first with a carrier oil, such as olive oil. A massage using essential oils can help to ease muscle tension alongside offering mental health benefits. Or for a more immersive experience, simply add a few drops to a warm bath for a restorative soak.

HE IS A WISE MAN WHO
DOES NOT GRIEVE
FOR THE THINGS WHICH
HE HAS NOT, BUT
REJOICES FOR THOSE
WHICH HE **HAS.**

EPICTETUS

Book a
reiki session

This alternative therapy is commonly referred to as energy healing. Said to involve the transfer of universal energy from the practitioner's palms to your body, proponents claim it can increase your life force energy, which in turn can improve your mental, spiritual and physical well-being. Many who undergo reiki healing report feeling a deep sense of relaxation and calm following the session.

Practise gratitude

By actively looking for and noticing things to feel grateful for, you will start to cultivate optimism and improve the quality of your life. In fact, research has found that expressing gratitude has a positive impact on almost all areas of well-being, including increasing happiness, improving self-esteem, strengthening relationships, deepening relaxation, boosting energy, improving sleep, promoting kindness and enhancing spirituality.

A good way to begin is to start keeping a short, daily gratitude journal – list the things you feel most grateful for at the end of each day. You could limit yourself to one or two things, or you could write down everything you have felt grateful for that day – the choice is yours. After several weeks, reflect on how this practice is altering your outlook on both yourself and the world around you.

Get creative

Losing yourself in a creative project can be deeply satisfying – numerous studies show that tapping into your creative side can do wonders for your mental health. Creativity can take many forms – painting, drawing, colouring, sculpting, sewing, knitting, baking, writing, singing, dancing, acting – so choose something that appeals to you and get stuck in. The good news is, you don't have to be an expert: the joy lies in the doing, as opposed to the finished outcome. So let loose and create!

Always be yourself.

Consider acupuncture

Several studies have shown that acupuncture is an effective treatment for mild depression, or those experiencing depression relating to a chronic medical illness. It involves the insertion of very fine needles into the skin at specific points in the body. Although it does not hurt, most people experience a mild ache, slight tingling, warmth or heaviness at the acupuncture points. Traditional Eastern medicine claims that acupuncture releases energy blockages or imbalances within the body; Western science has shown that it releases endorphins – the body's feel-good chemicals, which also act as natural painkillers – all of which might explain acupuncture's effectiveness.

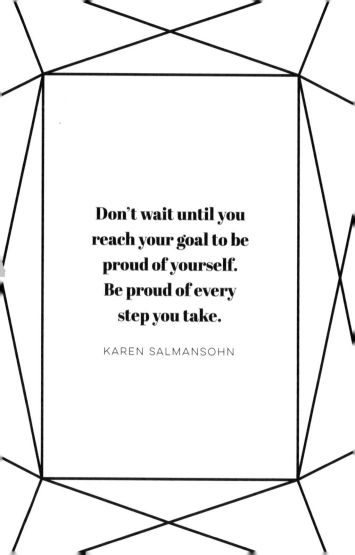

Don't wait until you reach your goal to be proud of yourself. Be proud of every step you take.

KAREN SALMANSOHN

GETTING PROFESSIONAL HELP

The previous chapters have described the many ways in which you can help yourself in times of mental distress, as well as how to cultivate good mental well-being. Of course, sometimes it may be necessary to seek professional guidance in order to access the correct support and give yourself the best chance of recovery. Asking for help can be uncomfortable and you may not be able to find the right words to open up, but letting someone know you need help shows strength.

GETTING
BETTER IS
NOT AN
OVERNIGHT
PROCESS.

TAKE THE
FIRST STEP

Realizing that there is an issue is the first big step, but often – with help, guidance and support – it can feel like a relief. The recognition that you are no longer going it alone – as well as the reassurance that you won't always feel this sad, empty or unhappy – can bring with it respite. If you've been hiding your feelings, you may have been experiencing huge pressure, alongside an expectation to act like you are "OK". Admitting that you are not can feel like a big weight has been lifted off your shoulders.

It's important to take things one step at a time, so you don't start feeling overwhelmed.

If you find you're still struggling after confiding in someone close to you, or chatting with someone on the other end of a helpline, the next step is to book an appointment with your doctor. There, you will be able to explain how you have been feeling and behaving to an understanding professional, in a safe and confidential environment. Your doctor may be able to diagnose your condition and discuss various treatments with you, or if they feel your needs are more complex, they may refer you to a specialist.

HEALING
TAKES TIME,
AND ASKING
FOR HELP IS A
COURAGEOUS
STEP.

MARISKA HARGITAY

Open up to one person

There are no rules when it comes to telling people about your mental health problem, although sharing it with someone close to you is a good way to enlist support. Starting by telling just one person can be less overwhelming. Of course, it will be difficult for you to predict how they will react, so try to keep an open mind and be considerate of their feelings. Be prepared for them to ask lots of questions. They might get upset, or even angry – it can sometimes be hard for people to hear. However they respond, remember that their reaction is not a reflection on you. You are doing a strong, brave thing by telling them.

Helplines and other services

If you are finding it difficult to open up to somebody in person – whether that's to a friend, family member or professional – don't worry. You are certainly not the only one who finds this uncomfortable. While some people find relief in sharing their innermost thoughts and feelings, not everyone finds it easy. If this is the case, you don't have to struggle on alone – there are plenty of opportunities to gain support and advice anonymously.

Helplines, such as The Samaritans, offer a safe space for you to talk through any worries, concerns or problems you may be experiencing. There is also a lot of help and advice available online. This includes websites and online forums, where you can chat anonymously with others. When looking for online support, it's important to be mindful of the source of the information you are accessing. Choose only reputable sites, such as registered charities. Responsible sites will normally contain trigger warnings before showing any content that might be upsetting to people in a vulnerable state. You might also like to consider apps to help you with self-care practices, such as mindfulness or meditation. These can help to keep you grounded in times of worry or anxiety.

THE BEST WAY
OUT IS ALWAYS
THROUGH.

ROBERT FROST

FORGIVE YOURSELF AND FORGIVE OTHERS.

EMERGENCY SUPPORT

If you're experiencing a mental health crisis right now, you will need to access immediate help. A mental health crisis could be suicidal feelings, but this is not the only time when you might need urgent support. It could be when you feel like you will start self-harming, in the midst of a panic attack, or during a manic episode. In short, you should seek support any time your mental health is at breaking point. If you feel you are in immediate danger – for example, if you are feeling suicidal – tell someone you trust as soon as possible or call a helpline (such as The Samaritans – see the resources section). Alternatively, you might need to make an emergency appointment with your doctor.

It's a good idea to make a plan in advance for how you would cope during a time of crisis, as it will help to keep you safe. Write down your personal action plan – the things you know help you. For example, who will you contact? What are the relevant helpline numbers? What acts of self-care could you take to make the moment feel more manageable? Keep this plan to hand, perhaps in your purse or wallet, to help you feel prepared and empowered.

**Ask for help,
not because you are weak,
but because you want
to remain strong.**

LES BROWN

PROGRESS IS PROGRESS, NO MATTER HOW SLOW. YOU'RE DOING GREAT.

CONCLUSION

Hopefully this book has helped you realize that it's perfectly normal to not feel OK sometimes. We all have days when we'd rather stay hidden under the covers than get up and face the day. At times like these, the best thing you can do is try a few self-care tips (whichever appeal the most to you at that particular moment) and give yourself a short break. You're human, and it's OK to do whatever you need to do to look after you for a while. But if those down days start turning into weeks (or even months), it's important to seek support. You don't have to go it alone – lots of people care about you (probably more than you realize). In time, and with the right guidance, you will start to feel more like yourself again. So hang in there – and never give up on yourself.

RESOURCES

For further help and information, you may find the following useful:

Anxiety UK: information, support and understanding for those living with anxiety disorders.
anxietyuk.org.uk

Beat: guidance and support for those with eating disorders, as well as their loved ones.
beateatingdisorders.org.uk

Campaign Against Living Miserably (CALM): leading a movement against male suicide.
thecalmzone.net

Drinkline: the UK's free, confidential national alcohol helpline.
0300 123 1110 (open weekdays 9 a.m. to 8 p.m.; weekends 11 a.m. to 4 p.m.)

LifeSIGNS: support, guidance and understanding around self-injury.
lifesigns.org.uk

Mind: support and advice to help empower anyone experiencing a mental health problem.
mind.org.uk

Switchboard: a listening and support service for LGBT+ people, via phone, email and instant messaging.
switchboard.lgbt

The Samaritans: a 24-hour free, confidential helpline, to support you whatever you're going through.
samaritans.org; 116 123; jo@samaritans.org / jo@samaritans.ie

For readers in the United States:

Anxiety and Depression Association of America: education, training and research for anxiety, depression and related disorders.
adaa.org

Mental Health America: promoting the overall mental health of all Americans.
mentalhealthamerica.net

National Institute of Mental Health: the lead federal agency for research on mental disorders.
nimh.nih.gov; 1-866-615-6464

National Suicide Prevention Lifeline: free, confidential support for people in distress.
suicidepreventionlifeline.org; 1-800-273-8255

To Write Love On Her Arms: supporting people struggling with depression, addiction, self-injury and suicide.
twloha.com

If you're interested in finding out more about our books, find us on Facebook at **Summersdale Publishers** and follow us on Twitter at **@Summersdale**.

www.summersdale.com

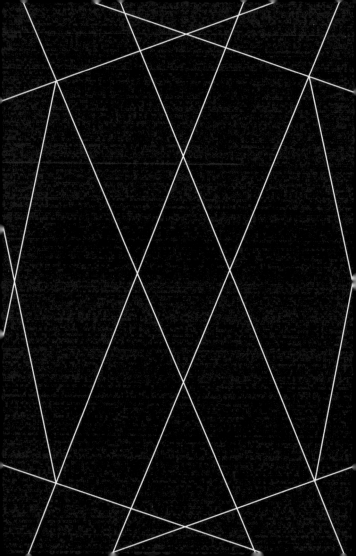